Chapter 1: The Power of Self-Aware
Chapter 2: The Power of Embracing
Chapter 3: The Power of Radical Acc
Chapter 4: The Power of Giving Up...
Chapter 5: Power of Imperfections.....
Chapter 6: Power of Environment 1
Chapter 7: Power of Forgiving 1
Chapter 8: The Power of Habits 1
Chapter 9: Power of Education 1
Chapter 10: The Power of Negativity 1
Chapter 11: Power of No Power 1
Afterword 1
References 1
Foreword 1

Foreword

About the Book

As I ventured into the world of self-help literature, I found myself pondering the necessity of formal expertise to make a meaningful contribution. My journey through mental illness, however, has equipped me with a wealth of personal experiences and coping mechanisms that I believe could offer solace and guidance to others navigating similar paths. I'm someone who's been through the wringer with mental illness, and through the ups and downs, I've picked up a few tricks along the way. This book? It's not your standard, textbook on mental health management. It's a collection of my own stories—intimate, unfiltered, and real. It's for anyone who prefers learning from lived experiences rather than clinical advice. But don't get me wrong, I've done my homework, researched extensively to back up my personal coping mechanisms with science, showing you that maybe, just maybe, they could work for you too. I need to be clear though: this book is not a replacement for professional help. That's a drum I'll beat over and over again.

This book is deeply personal, a mix of self-help and autobiography, detailing my own battles with managing mental health. I'm no therapist or psychiatrist. I'm the patient—someone who's been on the receiving end of their expertise. Diagnosed with GAD (generalized anxiety disorder) as well as MADD (mixed anxiety and depressive disorder), I've gathered a bunch of tried-and-tested tips, advice, and self-help guides that have worked for me. They might not work for everyone, but if they help even just one person feel a little less alone, then writing this book will have been worth it. This isn't a guide on how to manage your mental health professionally; it's about my journey of self-help and discovery, hoping to reach others who can relate, inspire those who can't, and share a slice of what life with anxiety really looks like.

My Unfiltered Story

It all started in my teenage years, holed up in a dark room with only my laptop for company. Finances were tight, and I used that as an excuse to avoid going outside, not realizing the toll it was taking on both my eyesight and my mental health. I kept to myself, distanced from classmates who were much older than me because I was homeschooled and later attended classes for the GED. My family situation was far from ideal, with an abusive alcoholic parent and an enabling one. It wasn't exactly a nurturing environment for a growing child.

By the time I reached my early teens, I had already begun to retreat inwardly, losing myself in a culture heavily influenced by social media and burdened by unrealistic expectations of appearance. The relentless pursuit of perfection and the need to conform to a specific ideal became suffocating. My struggles were further compounded by the turmoil in Myanmar due to the 2021 military coup, escalating my stress to unprecedented levels. The situation at home, marked by unresolved childhood trauma, unemployment, and toxic relationships—all exacerbated by the global pandemic—pushed me to the edge, manifesting in daily battles with suicidal thoughts. My anxiety reached a point where it triggered physical symptoms, such as psoriasis, a condition where the immune system, in an overzealous attempt to protect the body, mistakenly signals danger, leading to inflammation. This physical manifestation was a stark indicator of the profound connection between my emotional turmoil and physical health, signaling the urgent need for professional intervention.

After receiving diagnoses of Generalized Anxiety Disorder (GAD) and Mixed Anxiety and Depressive Disorder (MADD)—to which I initially responded with a half-hearted joke, "Oh wow, I am literally MADD!"—and recognizing symptoms akin to OCD, I felt truly acknowledged for the first time. It was as if I had been handed a key to decipher the chaos within my mind. Armed with this newfound understanding, I dedicated myself to mastering my mental health. Through trial and error, I not only learned valuable lessons but also experienced significant personal growth, evident in the healthy relationships I now maintain with myself and others.

Now, I stand before you, sharing my narrative through the pages of this book. It is my sincerest hope that by laying bare my heart and recounting both the victories and defeats in my battle with anxiety, I can offer you solace, guidance, or simply a sense of connection. This book is a tribute to the resilience we discover within ourselves in the face of anxiety, serving as a poignant reminder that even in our loneliest moments, we are never truly alone.

Chapter 1: The Power of Self-Awareness

Self-Reflection Through Journaling

Language is a powerful tool, not just for communication but as a mirror to our inner world. Even for those of us who don't consider ourselves linguistically inclined, the act of writing can unravel the complexities of our minds, laying our thoughts bare on paper. This process has become a lifeline for me, especially when my mind feels like a tangled mess of intrusive, anxious, and sometimes dark thoughts. The act of journaling has allowed me to sift through these thoughts, distinguishing the helpful from the harmful, and understanding the patterns that govern my mental landscape. This didn't happen overnight. Since 2016, journaling has been my constant companion, with a brief hiatus, but now it's a practice I don't see myself abandoning anytime soon. The goal was simple: unload my thoughts somewhere safe.

As I write, I constantly check in with myself. Am I being honest about my flaws, my insecurities, my feelings? There were times when I caught myself lying in my journal, which seemed ridiculous. After all, my journal was the one place where I could be unapologetically raw and real. Why mask the truth in a space meant for my eyes only? So, I made a pact to embrace brutal honesty in my entries, no matter how unsavory or "evil" the thoughts seemed. This practice of self-validation through writing has been transformative, bolstering my self-esteem and motivating me to continue on my path of self-improvement.

Journaling has become my go-to for processing emotions, whether it's the fallout from an argument, a rough day at work, or moments of insecurity. It's my safe space to express feelings without fear of judgment or the need to present a polished facade. Writing down my experiences has helped me recognize that my feelings, however negative, are valid and normal. It's a realization that has allowed me to accept parts of myself I used to hide, from anger and annoyance to vulnerabilities I was too proud to acknowledge.

This journey of self-awareness through journaling has revealed the multifaceted nature of my being—my strengths and weaknesses, my hopes and fears. It's a space where I can confront my regrets and commit to doing better next time, whether that means setting healthier boundaries or practicing self-compassion. Journaling has taught me about my behavior, thought patterns, and deepest desires, allowing me to affirm my humanity and recognize my inherent worth.

I've discovered that journaling can be a powerful tool for those who struggle to open up or fear being judged. It has certainly made me a better communicator, enabling me to express myself more clearly and calmly, even when conveying negative feelings. The act of journaling has improved not just my self-awareness but also how I interact with others, fostering more peaceful and productive conversations.

Journaling has become my most cherished habit, a testament to the healing power of putting pen to paper—or fingers to keyboard. It's a practice that offers immense growth, insight, and a unique form of companionship. Whether you prefer speaking into a recorder, typing on a device, or the traditional pen-and-paper method, the important thing is to start. This habit has been a cornerstone of my mental health management, a cathartic release that costs nothing but offers everything in return.

Expanding on the theme of journaling leading to self-reflection, I've discovered that this practice serves as a catalyst for profound personal insights and growth. Here are more detailed examples of how journaling has facilitated my journey of self-reflection:

Identifying Emotional Triggers

Through consistent journaling, I began to notice patterns in my emotional responses that I previously couldn't pinpoint. For instance, writing about days when my anxiety peaked, I traced many of these instances back to moments of feeling overwhelmed by tasks or interactions that reminded me of past failures. Seeing these patterns laid out in my own handwriting made it impossible to ignore the connections between certain events and my emotional responses. This realization led me to explore coping strategies specifically aimed at managing feelings of being overwhelmed, such as breaking tasks into smaller, more manageable steps and practicing mindfulness to stay present.

Confronting Insecurities

Journaling provided a safe space to confront my insecurities head-on. Writing about moments when I felt inadequate or comparing myself to others, I was able to dissect these feelings further. I asked myself why I felt this way and whether these insecurities were based on my own values or imposed by societal expectations. Over time, this practice helped me differentiate between the two and focus on building self-esteem around my own definitions of success and worth, rather than external validation.

Processing Relationship Dynamics

Writing about my interactions with friends, family, and colleagues allowed me to reflect on the dynamics of these relationships. For example, journaling about a disagreement with a friend helped me see my part in the conflict more clearly. It wasn't just about venting; it was about understanding my reactions, my friend's perspective, and the underlying issues that led to the disagreement. This self-reflection prompted me to initiate a conversation where we both could share our feelings openly, leading to a deeper, more understanding relationship.

Celebrating Personal Growth

Journaling isn't just for dwelling on challenges; it's also a powerful tool for recognizing and celebrating personal growth. By periodically reviewing past entries, I could see my progress over time. Moments that once seemed insurmountable were now just memories, and patterns of thought or behavior that I worked to change had evolved. This retrospection provided a sense of accomplishment and motivated me to continue setting and working towards personal goals.

Enhancing Self-Compassion

Perhaps one of the most significant outcomes of journaling has been the development of self-compassion. Writing about my experiences, especially those moments of failure or self-doubt, and then responding to myself with kindness and understanding, as I would to a friend, has been a powerful exercise. This practice helped me internalize a more compassionate voice, replacing self-criticism with empathy and understanding towards myself.

Through these examples, it's clear how journaling has been more than just a habit for me; it's been a journey of self-discovery and growth. By providing a space to explore my thoughts and feelings without judgment, journaling has led to greater self-awareness, emotional intelligence, and a deeper connection with my inner self.

Journaling Prompts to Get You Started

Gratitude List: Begin by listing three things you're grateful for today. This can shift your perspective and help cultivate a positive mindset.

Daily Reflections: Write about your day. What went well? What challenges did you face? How did you respond to those challenges?

Emotional Check-In: How are you feeling right now? Try to describe your emotions as precisely as possible. If you're feeling anxious, for example, explore what might be contributing to those feelings.

Stream of Consciousness: Set a timer for 5-10 minutes and write whatever comes to mind without editing or judging your thoughts. This can help you tap into deeper thoughts and feelings.

Sample Journal Entries

Gratitude Entry: "Today, I'm grateful for the sunny weather, my friend's supportive text message, and the delicious coffee I had this morning. These things brought me joy amidst a hectic day."

Daily Reflection: "Work was overwhelming today, with back-to-back meetings and a tight deadline. I noticed I felt anxious around midday. Taking a short walk during lunch helped me calm down. Tomorrow, I'll try to schedule a break between meetings for some breathing space."

Emotional Check-In: "I'm feeling unsettled tonight, possibly because of the unresolved argument with my partner. It's a mix of frustration and sadness. I need to communicate my feelings without placing blame."

Stream of Consciousness: "I'm worried about the presentation next week. Am I prepared enough? I keep doubting my capabilities, but I know I've done the work. Need to focus on positive outcomes and visualize success."

Chapter 2: The Power of Embracing Your Raw, Authentic Nature

Struggling with imperfections, fearing even the slightest mistakes, and the daunting worry of disappointing both yourself and those around you—if this resonates with you, you're likely familiar with the grip of anxiety. For me, much of this anxiety stemmed from a reluctance to confront and accept my imperfections, which I've now learned to see as my raw, authentic nature. This perspective shift has been nothing short of liberating.

Growing up, the Asian cultural and familial expectations surrounding appearance and behavior were suffocating. As a woman, I felt pressured to conform to ideals of being skinny, docile, and fair-skinned. My worth was seemingly conditional on these outward standards. In my teenage years, this led to a harmful association between my self-worth and my appearance. I wouldn't step outside unless I felt "perfect," obsessively checking my weight and covering any blemishes with makeup, exacerbating my skin issues in the process. The message was clear: my natural appearance, including my tanned skin, was not acceptable.

This internal struggle wasn't just about skin deep issues. Being outspoken and honest was seen as unbecoming of a girl, prompting me to mask my true feelings and adopt a more agreeable facade. This act of self-concealment only fueled my anxiety and intrusive thoughts, leading me to believe that revealing my true self would result in rejection and unlovability.

It was a profound realization that changed everything: I am beautiful in my own unique way. My honesty is my strength, and my vibrant energy is not something to be ashamed of, regardless of societal gender expectations. I began practicing affirmations, reminding myself of my beauty and worth, irrespective of others' opinions or preferences.

Scientific research supports the idea that accepting our vulnerabilities and imperfections can lead to greater well-being. According to studies on self-compassion, embracing our flaws without judgment encourages emotional resilience and reduces anxiety. This aligns with my experience; acknowledging and accepting my insecurities, rather than denying them, has fostered a deeper sense of self-compassion. Understanding the root causes of my insecurities, many of which were imposed by societal and cultural standards, has allowed me to shift my mindset and attitude towards a more self-compassionate outlook.

This journey of acceptance has not only heightened my self-compassion but has also significantly eased my anxiety. Denying my insecurities only perpetuated them, but accepting my authentic self has liberated me from the chains of perfectionism. I've learned to see my so-called flaws not as shortcomings but as facets of my unique individuality.

Now, when I catch myself being overly critical or envious of others, I pause and reflect: "Yes, I feel insecure, but what can I do next? How can I use this feeling as a stepping stone for self-improvement?" This approach of acknowledging and working through my insecurities is far more constructive than denial, which stems from ego and hinders personal growth.

Embracing my raw, authentic nature has proven to be a win-win strategy. Acceptance not only fosters self-compassion but also acts as a powerful antidote to anxiety. It's a reminder that I am worthy of love and belonging, just as I am, imperfections and all. This realization is not just a personal victory; it's a universal truth that can empower us all to live more authentically and freely.

Let's delve deeper into the transformative journey of embracing one's raw, authentic nature through specific examples from my life, illustrating how this practice of acceptance has fostered self-compassion and alleviated anxiety, supported by scientific insights.

Overcoming Beauty Standards

Before: I spent countless mornings scrutinizing my reflection, my heart sinking at the sight of any blemish or the number on the scale. The ritual of hiding my perceived flaws under layers of makeup, and the relentless pursuit of products promising fairer skin, became my norm. My self-esteem was tethered to these superficial standards, and any deviation plunged me into deep self-loathing.

After: One morning, I decided to face the world without the mask. It was terrifying but liberating. As I walked down the street, the anticipated judgment from others never came. Instead, I found kindness in strangers' smiles and realized that my fear of rejection was largely internal. This act of defiance against my ingrained insecurities was my first step toward self-acceptance. Research supports this shift, indicating that challenging societal beauty norms and embracing one's natural appearance can lead to improved body image and self-esteem (Cash & Smolak, 2011).

Speaking My Truth

Before: I often bit my tongue, holding back my opinions to fit the mold of what I was told a woman should be—agreeable and unobtrusive. This self-silencing led to a buildup of frustration and a sense of inauthenticity, feeding into my anxiety and feelings of worthlessness.

After: I began to express my thoughts and feelings openly, starting with small, safe groups where I felt supported. Each time I voiced my opinion, instead of the expected criticism, I found understanding and respect. This practice of authentic expression is supported by psychological research, which suggests that authenticity is closely linked to well-being and that self-expression can reduce stress and improve mental health (Ryan & Deci, 2001).

Accepting My Skin Tone

Before: I cringed at photos that showcased my tanned skin, a stark reminder of my deviation from the prized ideal of fairness within Asian culture. My insecurity was so profound that I avoided social gatherings and outdoor activities, fearing further darkening of my skin.

After: Inspired by role models who embraced their natural beauty, I started to question the standards I had internalized. I began to celebrate my skin tone, wearing colors that complemented it rather than hiding it. This shift not only boosted my confidence but also expanded my social world. Studies have shown that embracing one's natural physical attributes can lead to greater life satisfaction and lower levels of depression (Tiggemann & Slater, 2014).

Navigating Imperfections

Before: Any mistake, no matter how minor, would spiral me into a cycle of self-criticism and doubt, reinforcing my belief that I was fundamentally flawed.

After: I adopted a practice of writing down each mistake in my journal, not as a record of failure, but as a learning opportunity. This reflection helped me to see growth in every setback. The psychological concept of "growth mindset," popularized by Carol Dweck, resonates with this approach, suggesting that viewing challenges as opportunities for growth can enhance resilience and motivation.

The Power of Self-Compassion

Before: I harshly judged myself for any sign of vulnerability, seeing it as a weakness.

After: I learned to treat myself with the same kindness I would offer a friend in distress. When feelings of inadequacy surfaced, I responded with affirmations of my worth and reminders of my strengths. Research by Kristin Neff has shown that self-compassion can significantly reduce anxiety and depression, promoting a healthier relationship with oneself.

Personal goals, such as leading a meeting or presenting a project, using my insecurities as a checklist of achievements to tackle. This approach is supported by the concept of "beneficial self-doubt" in psychological research, suggesting that a moderate level of self-doubt can motivate individuals to prepare more thoroughly and perform more effectively (Leary, 2007).

This shift in mindset transformed my relationship with my insecurities. Instead of allowing them to dictate my self-worth, I used them as a compass for my personal development journey. By actively engaging with and working through my insecurities, I not only improved in the areas I once felt deficient but also bolstered my overall confidence and self-esteem.

These strategies, rooted in the power of embracing one's raw, authentic nature, highlight the dynamic process of personal growth. Through acknowledging imperfections, speaking one's truth, celebrating natural attributes, navigating setbacks as opportunities, practicing self-compassion, and using insecurity as motivation, we can foster a deeper, more compassionate understanding of ourselves. This journey, supported by scientific insights, showcases the transformative potential of self-acceptance, proving that our greatest challenges can indeed become our most powerful catalysts for change.

Chapter 3: The Power of Radical Acceptance

What are your flaws? The ugly truths you hesitate to acknowledge? Do you see yourself as selfish, overly dependent emotionally, or perhaps someone who pushes people away despite craving love? Are you masking your insecurities with a facade of confidence? Do you harbor resentment towards your family, despite societal norms dictating love and reverence towards them?

Being human involves accepting not only our external realities but also the internal ones—our thoughts, feelings, and behaviors that are far from perfect. Often, we suppress or deny what we perceive as "shameful" thoughts due to fear of judgment or self-reproach. I'm no stranger to this. There are undoubtedly subconscious thoughts and feelings I've repressed and unknowingly projected onto others.

Acceptance, famously known as the final stage of the five stages of grief, is arguably the most challenging to achieve. This difficulty extends beyond grief to encompass our emotions, thoughts, and daily approaches. Acceptance is a complex process in our brains. Even with seemingly minor issues, like a small acne spot or a minor health hiccup, our primal instinct is often denial. This gives us a false sense of control but merely postpones the inevitable confrontation with the issue, which is usually the harder part.

Admitting to this might feel akin to confessing a crime, but I, too, harbor deep insecurities and raw truths I was reluctant to face. For instance, my insecurities about my physical appearance—worrying about facial asymmetry or believing my cheeks too chubby. Realizing that denying and covering up these "flaws" did more harm than good was a pivotal moment. Accepting my appearance as it is, acknowledging that I deserve love regardless of how I look, was a crucial step. This mindset of radical acceptance has not only boosted my confidence but also reinforced the belief that I control who I let into my life.

Another harsh reality was my tendency towards emotional dependency in relationships, draining those I was close to. Acknowledging this wasn't easy, but doing so allowed me to change my behavior patterns. Instead of seeking validation from loved ones, I focused on self-improvement, socializing more, and setting healthy boundaries. Radical acceptance doesn't equate to condoning behavior; it means confronting reality to catalyze change.

The toughest pill to swallow was my feelings towards my family, especially my parents. Society often insists on familial love, but accepting my deep-seated resentment enabled me to prioritize my mental and physical health. Setting boundaries and acknowledging that biological ties don't dictate my concept of family were liberating steps.

So, how does one practice radical acceptance? For me, it meant prioritizing my inner state over others' perceptions, such as distancing myself from toxic family dynamics and acknowledging my flaws openly. Radical acceptance is about admitting the truth to oneself as a precursor to actionable change—whether that's setting boundaries, improving health, or advocating for oneself.

Scientific studies support the benefits of radical acceptance. For instance, research on acceptance and commitment therapy (ACT) shows that embracing our thoughts and feelings without judgment can significantly reduce psychological distress and increase psychological flexibility (Hayes et al., 2006). Furthermore, a mindset of acceptance has been linked to better stress management and overall well-being (Shallcross et al., 2010).

Radical acceptance is just the beginning. It's the acknowledgment of our reality that sets the stage for transformative action. Surrounding ourselves with inspiring individuals, especially those who've navigated similar challenges, can provide motivation and a sense of community. Remember, radical acceptance is a mental state, a necessary step before action. It's through subsequent actions that we witness the most significant changes in both our internal and external worlds.

Let's take a specific example using my own life story to show you how one could practice radical acceptance.

Embracing Radical Acceptance: Confronting Family Dynamics

One of the most profound truths I had to face through radical acceptance was my feelings towards my family, especially my parents. Contrary to societal beliefs that preach unconditional love for one's family, I found myself in a tumultuous relationship with mine. Acknowledging that I harbored resentment was a challenge;

society often denies the possibility of such feelings, insisting that "they are your family, after all." However, this denial was at odds with my inner truth—that I deeply resented them. This denial led me to tolerate abusive behavior, both physical and emotional, and neglect my own mental and physical health. It trapped me in a cycle of trying to "fix" my family dynamics and choosing partners who mirrored these unresolved issues, perpetuating a cycle of dysfunction.

Only through the lens of radical acceptance was I able to break free from this cycle. Accepting the stark reality that I harbored negative feelings towards my family allowed me to establish necessary boundaries. This acceptance wasn't about condoning their behavior but rather acknowledging that I couldn't change the past or their actions. It empowered me to prioritize my own well-being and create a life aligned with my values, independent of societal expectations or familial obligations.

Practicing Radical Acceptance

For me, radical acceptance involved a conscious decision to prioritize my internal well-being over external perceptions. This meant physically distancing myself from my family, limiting communication to essential interactions, and owning up to my vulnerabilities, such as acknowledging my insecurities and my tendency towards emotional dependency. This process underscores the power of vulnerability, a theme I shall delve deeper into in later chapters. Radical acceptance acts as a catalyst for personal transformation, prompting us to confront our "ugly truths" and embark on a journey towards authentic self-improvement.

The steps towards embracing radical acceptance and initiating change are multifaceted and time consuming. So, don't expect an overnight change. They include setting firm boundaries, focusing on physical and mental health, practicing meditation and mindfulness, cultivating the right social environment, and advocating for oneself. This approach shifts behavior patterns, leading to a positive change in thought processes and overall mindset. This approach was personal to mine - whatever approach that you know is right for you, is going to be your personal approach, to which I can not advise you specifically to do but only you shall know upon your self reflection.

A very important aspect of radical acceptance is the contemplation of the consequences of denial. Asking oneself, "What happens if I don't accept these truths about myself and fail to take action?" helps clarify the path forward. If the drawbacks of denial outweigh the benefits, it's a clear indication that acceptance and subsequent action are necessary.

The Impact of Radical Acceptance

Radical acceptance is more than just acknowledging difficult truths; it's about understanding that you're capable of growth beyond these challenges. It's a foundational step in the process of personal evolution, leading to a healthier, more authentic life. By accepting the reality of our situations and our feelings, we can make informed decisions about how to proceed, fostering a sense of empowerment and self-determination.

This approach is supported by psychological research, which suggests that acceptance of one's circumstances and emotions is linked to better emotional regulation and psychological well-being (Hayes, Strosahl, & Wilson, 1999). It enables individuals to face their issues directly, reducing the psychological distress associated with avoidance and denial.

In essence, radical acceptance is about taking control of your narrative and making choices that align with your true self. It's a commitment to navigating life's complexities with honesty and courage, paving the way for genuine healing and growth.

Remember, radical acceptance serves as the mental groundwork before you reach the action stage. It's in the action stage where you truly begin to make and witness significant changes.

Chapter 4: The Power of Giving Up

Give up. Yes, you've read that right. We're commonly taught to think that giving up should be our last resort when we're pursuing something we desire. I strongly challenge this notion. Far from being a sign of defeat, choosing to give up can actually symbolize a victory. It creates space for the aspects of our lives that are genuinely meant for us. The art of letting go, when mastered—knowing precisely when and how—embodies true courage.

Let me share a story about a friend of mine. He was over the moon after meeting a woman he believed was the love of his life, just a few days into their acquaintance. His infatuation was so intense that he couldn't savor the moments at his own birthday party, preoccupied with thoughts of her—despite her absence, excused by her being "too busy" to attend. Things took a turn when she asked him for a substantial sum of money, blaming poor "budgeting" skills. Despite her being 34, my friend defended her, convinced she simply didn't know any better. Yet, as the woman's behavior escalated to emotional and physical abuse, it became painfully clear to everyone but him: he was in a toxic relationship. Thankfully, he got out of it at the end at the very first physical abuse.

This narrative is all too familiar. Many find themselves trapped in harmful relationships due to various reasons: perhaps fear of being alone, lack of experience, familiarity with bad experiences, emotional manipulation, a refusal to let go, or even ego—believing they're immune to such situations. This story expresses the difficulty many face in recognizing when it's time to walk away.

Victims, often kind-hearted or lacking in experiences, fail to foresee the potential harm, hoping against hope that the other person will change for the better—a hope that is frequently exploited.

Choosing to let go, especially when clear signals emerge, is not only beneficial for one's mental health but, as in my friend's case, unfortunately, can be crucial for physical well-being too. This isn't to suggest that letting go is a sign of weakness. On the contrary, it's about acknowledging that sometimes, we may not recognize the right moment to step back. This realization highlights the importance of being attuned to our surroundings, understanding who our true allies are, and discerning the environments that best support our well-being—a theme to be explored further in upcoming chapters.

Scientific studies support the notion that disengaging from toxic relationships can lead to significant improvements in mental health. Research indicates that individuals who successfully remove themselves from harmful social contexts experience lower levels of stress and higher self-esteem (Frazier et al., 2009). Moreover, the act of letting go can foster a sense of empowerment and personal growth, reinforcing the idea that our well-being often hinges on our ability to make difficult but necessary decisions (Sbarra & Emery, 2005).

In essence, the power of letting go is not about accepting defeat but rather about making a strategic choice for our own good. It's about recognizing when our persistence is no longer serving us and making the brave decision to open ourselves up to new possibilities, growth, and ultimately, a life that aligns more closely with our true selves.

Growing up, I always wondered why my mother wouldn't leave my problematic father, who often struggled with drug abuse, alcoholic tendencies, and even violent behavior. This led to emotional abuse and scars, resulting in my mother resorting to reactive abuse. "If only she had given him up, her life would have been better." I realized that my mother, raised in a traditional and conservative society, was fearful of losing her one and only husband. To her, this meant losing her entire family and failing as a person; a woman who couldn't maintain a good relationship. In the tradition she was raised, it was considered a failure not to endure a husband's issues, no matter how problematic, for the sake of family unity and maintaining a good facade as dictated by cultural expectations. Although I could understand her reasoning and fear of giving up on something or someone she had invested most of her life in, the fear of starting over, or fear of judgment from others - the root was fear - I still couldn't see why she couldn't choose the option to give up. To me, possibly still naive, it seems like the best choice. I don't have a say in how anybody lives their life, so I can only take a life lesson from my mother, who has such trouble giving up and being consumed by the fear and anxiety that comes from giving up. Letting go of people or situations that are bad for us doesn't mean we failed but rather that we are on the right path with mistakes to learn from not to repeat even more so. In fact, it's a brave and good thing to do for ourselves and in my mother's case, she is not so fortunate.

Think about when you finally leave a job that makes you unhappy. Letting go feels freeing, just like that. But sometimes, we don't immediately feel happy after we let go of bad things or people. We humans are complex beings with complex emotions and it is important to validate your own emotions that mixed emotions which come after making the right choice is a normal emotion. We might feel unsure or even regretful, even though we know it was the right choice. It's important to give yourself time to feel happy about your decision to let go of the wrong things or people at the right time.

Yet, letting go isn't always straightforward. What if leaving a toxic relationship or job isn't feasible due to financial constraints or family responsibilities? In these instances, establishing boundaries becomes essential. Determining when and how you engage with challenging individuals or situations, and understanding that their reactions to your boundaries are their responsibility, not yours, can create a manageable environment.

Identifying what to let go can sometimes be challenging. In my personal journey, I realized that my tendency to people-please, initially a survival tactic, was severely undermining my self-esteem. Every yeses to unwanted requests and every unvoiced opinion in favor of appeasing others only served to reinforce my belief that my needs and opinions were secondary. This was painfully apparent in a toxic relationship where my attempts to express my feelings were met with gaslighting, eroding my sense of reality and self-worth. Recognizing that people-pleasing was a boundaryless path, I understood that I was the only one who could put an end to it. Embracing the act of letting go became the most respectful and liberating choice for my mental well-being.

I've come to realize that the ability to be disliked is, in essence, the ability to respect myself. Take a moment to reflect: Do I genuinely like everyone in my life? Every single person? If it's impossible for you to hold everyone in high regard, how can you expect universal approval in return? Rather than striving to meet an unattainable goal, finding comfort in the possibility of being disliked signifies that you're on the right path. It means you're letting go of others' opinions and placing a higher value on your own self-respect and views about yourself, which are infinitely more crucial.

This understanding liberates us from the chains of constant approval-seeking. When we stop trying to be everything to everyone, we start to honor our authenticity and values. This shift in perspective is not just about embracing our true selves but also about recognizing the strength in our convictions. By prioritizing our self-respect over the need to be universally liked, we foster a deeper sense of self-worth and personal integrity. Indeed, why should we aim to be agreeable at all times? Embrace originality in your thoughts and stand firm in your convictions. It's far more rewarding to be appreciated by the right people for your authentic self than to be liked by many for a persona that isn't truly yours. I personally wouldn't want that sort of personality crisis only fore-triggering my anxiety.

Scientific research supports the importance of self-acceptance and the psychological benefits of not relying on external validation for self-esteem. Studies have shown that individuals who base their self-worth on internal values rather than external approval experience greater life satisfaction and mental well-being (Crocker & Park, 2004). This approach aligns with the principles of self-determination theory, which emphasizes the role of autonomy and the pursuit of personal goals as key drivers of psychological health (Ryan & Deci, 2000).

A significant portion of my anxiety comes from feeling out of control. Questions like "What if others judge me for my speech or style?" or "What if my partner is unfaithful or secretly manipulating me?" haunt me. This desire for control, to steer the course of my life, paradoxically leads to behaviors that diminish my well-being: mistrust in relationships, self-criticism that erodes my confidence, and a cycle of errors followed by harsh self-judgment.

Yet, I've discovered that giving up control can be liberating, anchored by the mantra: "you are not missing out on anything you are meant to experience." The belief that we can control every aspect of our lives is nothing but an absolute delusion. When thinking about my five-year plan, I might pretend to have clarity, but honestly, I'm as uncertain about that as I am about my dinner plans. Life teaches us that much is beyond our control, a principle deeply embedded in the philosophy of Stoicism.

Stoicism, an ancient Greek philosophy, teaches the value of understanding what is within our control and accepting what is not. Stoics believe that while we can't control external events, we can control our perceptions, reactions, and internal states. This approach to life is not about passivity but about focusing our energy on our own actions, attitudes, and ethical living. Studies in psychology echo the Stoic view, demonstrating that individuals who distinguish between controllable and uncontrollable aspects of life tend to have better mental health outcomes. Psychological flexibility, a concept studied extensively, illustrates that adapting to life's uncontrollable aspects can lead to improved well-being and reduced anxiety (Kashdan & Rottenberg, 2010). Furthermore, adopting a Stoic attitude has been linked to resilience, life satisfaction, and emotional stability (Seligman, Steen, Park, & Peterson, 2005).

Stoicism encourages us to focus on our attitude, mindset, and how we choose to communicate and engage in healthy habits. By doing so, we align ourselves with what we can control, fostering a sense of inner peace and resilience against life's unpredictabilities.

Embracing Stoicism and the act of letting go transforms the way we navigate life. It teaches us to accept the unpredictability of life, focusing instead on personal growth, ethical living, and cultivating a tranquil mind. This philosophical approach does not eliminate challenges but equips us with the tools to face them more peacefully, reminding us that our power lies not in controlling the external world but in mastering our internal one.

Simply concluded, the key to successfully letting go and giving up lies in asking yourself: "Will my life improve by giving up on this?" If most of the evidence points to 'yes,' then it's time to make that brave decision.

Chapter 5: Power of Imperfections

I never saw myself as a perfectionist until I faced the truth—I was one, indeed. I just didn't want to acknowledge being labeled with the negative connotations of perfectionism. This very denial highlighted a perfectionist trait: the reluctance to be linked with any form of imperfection. Anxiety would grip me over small details, like my hair not looking just right, prompting me to avoid social events, or the fear that I wasn't articulate enough to be deemed "smart" or lovable. Deep down, I recognized this stemmed from my family's lack of recognition for my achievements, leading me to believe that only perfection, like scoring top marks or winning national chess competitions, could earn me love and attention.

However, this type of family neglect was beyond my control and didn't define my worthiness of being loved. Such realizations come with life's blend of failures and successes. This perfectionist mindset only amplified my anxiety, revealing perfectionism as an illusion and a misguided belief in total control. Growing up, I dreamed of a perfect life: numerous friends, marriage by 25, a stable job post-graduation, and a loving relationship with my first boyfriend. Yet, life had other plans, offering me harsh but invaluable lessons.

Embracing imperfection became a beautiful journey. My first relationship, far from ideal, turned out to be highly toxic, serving as a stark reminder that life is not always as perfect as we hope. The military coup in Myanmar and subsequent unemployment after university threw me into turmoil but taught me life's imperfections. I once believed fair skin was the epitome of beauty, influenced by toxic societal norms, but I've grown to love my tanned skin, seeing it as beautiful as any other. It was through navigating these rough waters—enduring a toxic relationship, facing unemployment, and identifying my true supporters—that I learned to value the lessons imperfection offers. As I continued to face life's imperfections, I adopted a "bring it on" attitude towards challenges.

Embracing my unique life story, with its ups and downs, has shaped me into the person I am today: strong, resilient, and educated by tough times. Accepting my imperfections has not only boosted my self-confidence but also led me to discover new values.

Of course, learning to embrace my imperfections wasn't a straightforward journey; it required a great deal of learning. This included educating myself, finding role models who could distinguish right from wrong, and engaging in a lot of psycho-education and self-reflection. So, if you were to ask me now whether I'm still a perfectionist, I'd be dishonest if I claimed I wasn't. I probably am, but I like to think I've transformed into a perfectionist with a healthier outlook, rather than clinging to the unhealthy tendencies of before.

Embracing imperfectionism and navigating through life's complexities, including cultural identity and familial dysfunction, have been profound journeys of growth and self-discovery for me. Here's a comprehensive look at how I've navigated these experiences, integrating the steps towards embracing imperfectionism with the challenges and triumphs of my personal journey:

Choosing the Right Role Models and Overcoming Familial Dysfunction

Before: Familial conflicts and lack of support left me craving stability, seeing perfectionism as the only solution to being loved.

After: By seeking therapy and surrounding myself with a chosen family of supportive friends, I learned to separate my self-worth from my family's dysfunction and separate the idea of being perfect and being worthy of love aren't equivalent.

Psycho-Education and Embracing a Multifaceted Identity

Before: My bicultural identity and family turmoil contributed to deep-seated anxiety and self-doubt.

After: Engaging in psycho-education, I began to view my complex identity not as a burden but as a badge of honor, learning that my diverse experiences offered unique insights and empathy towards others.

Self-Reflection

Regular self-reflection, through journaling and meditation, has been key in understanding how my experiences have shaped me. It allowed me to critically examine my perfectionist tendencies and their roots in my cultural and familial experiences, leading to a more compassionate view of myself.

Embracing Vulnerability

Opening up about my struggles with cultural identity and familial issues has fostered deeper connections and taught me the value of authenticity. Vulnerability has been a gateway to genuine relationships and self-acceptance.

Celebrating Small Wins

Acknowledging achievements, regardless of their size, has helped me recognize the value of my journey, including the lessons learned from navigating cultural divides and familial challenges. Celebrating these moments reinforces my growth beyond perfectionism.

Self-Compassion

Treating myself with kindness, especially when confronting the imperfections of my cultural identity and family dynamics, has been transformative. Self-compassion has been a critical factor in healing and building resilience.

Embracing Imperfectionism in Life's Challenges

The realization that life's imperfections, such as toxic relationships and the impact of political turmoil, like the military coup in Myanmar, are not failures but opportunities for growth. These experiences have taught me invaluable lessons about resilience and the beauty of imperfection.

Chapter 6: Power of Environment

Creating a nurturing external environment is crucial for your well-being, regardless of whether you're fully aware of its impact. Imagine being surrounded by people who don't support your dreams and goals. This could lead you to believe that your ideas and aspirations are insignificant. On the flip side, a supportive circle can boost your self-confidence and encourage you to chase after what you genuinely desire in life. The key to identifying whether you're in the right environment correlates with how well you understand your emotions and how you perceive others' judgments around you.

It's important to recognize that environments come in two types: internal and external. Your internal environment consists of your thoughts and mindsets, which drive your actions and shape who you are. The external environment involves the people around you, their opinions about you, and how they treat you, all of which influence your actions and self-perception.

Your habits significantly impact your internal environment. Daily activities, which might seem trivial, play a major role in shaping your mental health and well-being. Regularly assessing whether your actions are beneficial or harmful is crucial for maintaining a healthy mindset.

For instance, my struggle with anxiety taught me the importance of recognizing and modifying certain habits. Spending too much time on my phone, aimlessly scrolling through social media, or being unproductive can worsen my anxiety. It's vital to identify and limit such behaviors to create a more positive internal environment.

Building a positive internal environment is a process that involves nurturing your mental, emotional, and psychological well-being. It's about creating a space within yourself where you feel at peace, supported, and motivated. Here's an expanded guide on how to build a good internal environment:

Eliminating Negative Habits and Setting Boundaries

Identifying negative habits requires introspection and honesty. For instance, consider the time spent on activities that drain your energy without providing real value, such as scrolling through social media or procrastinating. The key to change lies in recognizing these patterns and understanding their triggers.

Actionable Strategy: Implement a 'habit audit' by keeping a journal for a week. Note down your daily activities and how they make you feel. Highlight those that contribute to negativity or anxiety. Gradually replace these with healthier alternatives that align with your goals and values. For example, replace social media time with reading or a hobby that nurtures your creativity and sense of accomplishment.

Daily Habit Audit Example

Day 1:

Morning:

Activity: Scrolling through social media immediately after waking up.

Mood/Impact: Felt overwhelmed and anxious about the day ahead.

Alternative: Tomorrow, try meditating for 5 minutes upon waking instead.

Afternoon:

Activity: Skipped lunch to work through a deadline.

Mood/Impact: Became irritable and struggled to focus later in the afternoon.

Alternative: Schedule a 15-minute break for lunch regardless of workload to maintain energy levels.

Evening:

Activity: Watched TV while eating dinner.

Mood/Impact: Felt disconnected and not fully relaxed.

Alternative: Focus on eating without distractions and then spend some time reading.

A study by Oulasvirta, Rattenbury, Ma, and Raita (2012) in "Personal and Ubiquitous Computing" discusses the concept of 'habit breaking' in the context of information technology use, suggesting that awareness and replacement of habitual behaviors can significantly improve personal well-being.

Practicing Self-Compassion

Self-compassion is not just about being kind to yourself in moments of failure or distress; it's about integrating this kindness into your daily self-talk and actions. It's recognizing that imperfection is part of the human experience and that every mistake is a step towards growth.

Actionable Strategy: Start a self-compassion diary. Each day, write down moments when you were hard on yourself, and reframe these thoughts with kindness and understanding. For instance, if you criticize yourself for a mistake at work, write down what you learned from the experience and how it can help you improve. Additionally, engage in self-care practices that promote mental and physical well-being, such as regular exercise, healthy eating, and sufficient sleep, which are foundational to self-compassion. Research by Neff and Germer (2013) in "Clinical Psychology Review" shows that self-compassion exercises can lead to increased emotional resilience, reduced stress, and a greater capacity to handle life's challenges.

Self compassion diary example:

Event: I made a mistake at work today.

How I feel about it: I am a failure.

Evidence for my feelings: maybe, everyone judged me and thinks I am incapable.

Evidence against my feelings: I usually don't make a mistake today. The mistake I made isn't that big.

Action-able steps: I can apologize if I need to and if not, I can move on and do better next time. Let's practice meditation and talk with trusted loved ones to feel better.

Self affirmation: one mistake doesn't fine my worth or my capability. I can't change what happened but I can do my best next time and my best is all that matters.

Identifying and Managing Anxiety Triggers

Anxiety triggers can be subtle and varied, from specific social situations to broader concerns about health, relationships, or the future. Identifying these triggers is the first step towards managing them effectively.

Actionable Strategy: Keep an anxiety trigger diary. Note when your anxiety spikes and what was happening at the time. Look for patterns. For example, if checking social media first thing in the morning leads to increased anxiety, modify your routine to include a positive activity instead, like meditation or a short walk.Incorporate grounding techniques into your daily routine, not just when you're anxious. This can make them more effective when you really need them. Techniques such as the 5-4-3-2-1 method, where you engage all your senses to ground yourself in the present, can be practiced anywhere and anytime to cultivate a habit of mindfulness. A study by Polk, Schoendorff, Webster, and Olaz (2016) in "Journal of Contextual Behavioral Science" highlights the effectiveness of mindfulness and acceptance-based practices, including grounding techniques, in managing anxiety and stress, demonstrating their value in improving mental health.

By delving deeper into these steps and incorporating them into your daily life, you can significantly enhance your internal environment. This not only helps in managing anxiety and stress but also in building a resilient, compassionate, and joyful inner world.

By adopting these strategies, you can cultivate a healthier internal environment, laying the foundation for a more contented and fulfilling life. Remember, your internal environment is your lifelong companion; nurturing it with kindness, awareness, and mindful practices is one of the most rewarding investments you can make.

90/10 Principle

Having delved into the intricacies of fostering a nurturing internal environment, we now turn our attention to the external factors and how they can be optimized. It's a common misconception that our external environment is beyond our control. While there are limits, we indeed have significant influence over whom we allow into our lives. The impact of our external environment is more profound than many of us realize. As social creatures, our behaviors, emotions, and thoughts are heavily influenced by our interactions with others. Environments lacking support or, worse, that are abusive, can severely damage our self-esteem and escalate anxiety levels. It's not solely the negative actions or words of others that contribute to an unhealthy external environment; sometimes, the issue lies in the lack of compatibility with our well-being. Consider, for example, a friend of mine who is loyal and shares similar values, including a commitment to self-improvement and a shared history of childhood trauma. Despite these positive traits, this friend's inability to respect boundaries and emotional dependency creates a significant source of anxiety for me. Although 10% of this friendship aligns with my values, the remaining 90% is detrimental, leading me to the conclusion that I cannot accept this external environment.

This 90/10 principle is applicable to positive external environments as well. It raises the question: if someone embodies 90% of what we desire but lacks 10%, should we let go of them because of our anxiety? The answer is a resounding no. Perfection is unattainable, both in our external environment and in life generally. What is essential is finding a balance between what internal and external influences we accept (flaws) and those we draw inspiration from (motivations).

Creating a robust and positive external environment, through careful selection of the people in our lives, has been instrumental in managing my anxiety. I am fortunate to have friends who not only support my aspirations but are also great listeners, respect personal boundaries, and serve as sources of inspiration. Observing individuals who successfully balance work and play motivates me and, in turn, helps alleviate my anxiety by providing reliable support.

The significance of a supportive external environment cannot be overstated, especially in the context of personal development and anxiety alleviation. Reflecting on my own experiences, I grew up with little support for my ambitions, leading me to doubt my aspirations. However, upon meeting individuals who believed in my dreams and demonstrated the possibilities for personal growth, I was encouraged to pursue my goals fearlessly. This transformation underscores the power of a positive external environment in overcoming self-doubt and pursuing one's dreams without fear of judgment.

Scientific studies reinforce the importance of a supportive external environment. Research on social support has consistently shown its positive impact on mental health, including reduced anxiety and depression symptoms. For instance, a study published in the "Journal of Personality and Social Psychology" found that individuals with strong social support networks were better equipped to manage stress and exhibited lower levels of psychological distress. Similarly, research in "Health Psychology" highlights the role of positive interpersonal relationships in enhancing well-being and resilience against stress. These studies underscore the critical role of our external environment in shaping our mental health and overall quality of life, validating the personal experiences shared in this narrative.

Chapter 7: Power of Forgiving

Throughout the chapters, I have mentioned family issues that have significantly impacted my anxiety and well-being. My focus on family is rooted in the understanding that this is where my anxiety originates; a dysfunctional and abusive environment during critical developmental years is not to be underestimated. It's quite apparent how such a family environment can mold a child into someone who grows up anxious, fearful, and distrustful of the world around them. My initial reaction was deep-seated resentment towards my family members, making the notion of forgiveness seem like an insurmountable challenge. "Why should I forgive them?" I questioned, equating forgiveness with conceding defeat to those who had caused immense emotional pain and stifled my personal growth.

However, my journey has led me to view forgiveness through a new lens, though it has been a lengthy and ongoing process. I've come to realize that forgiveness isn't about acknowledging defeat but rather recognizing the harm others have caused us and choosing to love and respect ourselves enough to move beyond it. It's about seeing people for who they truly are, not who we wanted or expected them to be.

For instance, the practice of forgiveness opened my eyes to my unrealistic expectations of my parents. It's not about faulting ourselves for our high expectations but rather confronting the reality of where we were in our lives and who these people truly are—be it as a child who believed their parents could do no wrong or as a teenager who idealized a romantic partner. This process of acceptance and letting go of unmet expectations is complex and requires a degree of maturity and radical acceptance that I continue to work on

Reflecting on our own lives reveals that those we need to forgive often hurt us during crucial life stages. It's likely that our disappointment stemmed from unmet expectations, leading to difficulties in forgiveness. Recognizing people for their true actions and words, rather than our expectations, is a crucial step in this process. For example, understanding that my parents prioritized their relationship over their children was a difficult truth to accept, but it was essential for moving towards forgiveness.

Forgiveness does not imply defeat; rather, it's a path to reducing anxiety and focusing on the present. It's about seeing the limitations within other people as well as within ourselves, and accepting them. By forgiving and setting boundaries, we not only protect our peace but also make room for healthier relationships. Adjusting our expectations and learning from these experiences can bring a sense of peace and reduce anxiety, acknowledging that not everyone will meet our expectations due to differing values or simply being different—and that's okay.

Supporting this personal journey, scientific studies have demonstrated the profound impact of forgiveness on mental health. Research published in the Journal of Health Psychology has shown that forgiveness is associated with lower levels of anxiety, depression, and stress. Similarly, a study in the Journal of Consulting and Clinical Psychology found that forgiveness interventions significantly improve emotional well-being. These findings highlight the benefits of forgiveness, not only as a means of personal growth but also as a strategy for enhancing mental health.

Dwelling on painful experiences by harboring unforgiveness only serves to perpetuate our unhappiness, which is counterintuitive to our ultimate goal of achieving less anxiety and greater happiness. Holding onto resentment and reliving past hurts can trap us in a cycle of negative emotions and stress, directly impacting our mental health and well-being. This cycle not only hinders our ability to move forward but also keeps us anchored to the very experiences we wish to overcome.

Scientific studies demonstrate the detrimental effects of clinging to negative emotions. Research in the field of psychology has shown that chronic anger and unforgiveness are linked to increased anxiety levels, stress, higher blood pressure, and other health issues that can contribute to a decrease in overall life satisfaction and well-being. Conversely, embracing forgiveness can lead to improved mental health outcomes, including reduced anxiety, depression, and stress levels.

Forgiveness, then, is not about condoning wrongdoing or forgetting the pain caused by others. Rather, it's an act of self-compassion and liberation. It's a conscious decision to release ourselves from the burden of past hurts, allowing us to redirect our energy towards healing and positive growth. By choosing forgiveness, we open the door to inner peace, which is essential for our happiness and mental health.

Forgiveness allows us to realign with what truly matters to us. It teaches us to practice gratitude for even the bad experiences, as they clarify what we genuinely don't want in our lives. Forgiveness is about taking control, setting boundaries, and choosing who we spend our time with based on how they treat us. Moving beyond victimhood and the desire for revenge, and instead focusing on living life on our own terms, is perhaps the most significant benefit forgiveness offers. Living peacefully, according to our values and desires, having freewill to what serves us, is the ultimate testament to the power of forgiveness.

Chapter 8: The Power of Habits

In the introduction of this book, I discussed how isolating myself in my room not only intensified my anxiety levels but also led me to become socially isolated and anxious. This detrimental habit became a significant trigger for my anxiety. Though we may often overlook the importance of habits, they are crucial in fighting anxiety.

My battle with anxiety and depression was so intense that I resorted to heavy dosages of medication. However, despite the medication, I noticed no improvement in my mood or anxiety levels. Instead, I felt perpetually numb due to the medication's sedative side effects. I realized I needed to start someplace more natural such as my habits. While I recognize the benefits of anxiety and depression medications, I personally prefer not to rely on them for managing my mental health. I believe in the possibility of natural recovery through living a life enriched with positive habits, which is precisely how I overcame deep depression and severe anxiety, even when they pushed me towards suicidal thoughts.

Allow me to share a personal example. Having a nurturing external environment led me to frequently engage in nature hikes, jungle explorations, and refreshing swims in waterfalls. This routine was a stark contrast to my teenage years, spent indoors, glued to my laptop screen until 5 am, trapped in a cycle of crippling anxiety and insomnia. Now, my days start at 6 am with meditation, followed by a productive workday, socializing with friends, and quality time with loved ones. My previous habits of staying up late, excessive screen time, and social isolation had fueled my anxiety and insomnia. Today, I am motivated, inspired, an early riser, driven by personal goals and curiosity. Frankly, I never imagined enjoying early mornings and living without the burden of anxiety. How did I achieve this transformation? Simply put, by changing my habits.

We often know which habits we need to discard and which ones to adopt; however, the challenge lies in taking action. Lack of motivation and support can hinder our progress. The first step in my journey to change my habits involved listing my daily routines for two weeks, noting how each activity made me feel and its importance on a scale from 1 (least important or most negative) to 5 (most important and positive). This method, previously mentioned, was instrumental in identifying the habits I needed to change. Habits like staying up late, self-isolation, high screen time, and lack of social and outdoor activities were exacerbating my anxiety and needed to be replaced.

However, simply deciding to change wasn't enough. For example, trying to wake up at 5 am when I was accustomed to going to bed at that time was unrealistic. I had to start slow, gradually adjusting my waking hours from 1 pm to eventually 6 am. Unlike some habits that required a gradual approach, others, such as self-isolation, could be addressed more directly. I pushed myself to go outside, ignoring fears of negative outcomes or judgment, and surrounded myself with people who embodied the habits I aspired to develop.

Participating in social events with little to no screen time, engaging in nature walks, and exploring new places with a loved one who shared my curiosity helped eliminate my habit of staying up late. Reading more and dedicating time to personal projects and self-education further alleviated my anxious thoughts. Within 3-4 months, the numbness and depression began to fade, healed by natural activities and the transition from detrimental to beneficial habits.

Although I still face challenges with certain habits, like excessive screen time or self-isolation, I remind myself of the negative feelings associated with these behaviors and push myself to break free. Whenever I feel demotivated, I ask myself, "Will this activity make me feel better in the end?" If the answer is yes, I compel myself to act, usually feeling better as a result. Even in instances where the outcome isn't as expected, such as an unsatisfying social interaction, I consider it a victory over remaining isolated with my laptop. This journey has taught me the transformative power of habits in the healing process.

Chapter 9: Power of Education

I've discovered that reading is not only a source of knowledge and intellectual fulfillment but also a significant anxiety-reducing activity. It has a calming effect on my mind and emotions, serving my emotional well-being positively. Through reading, I've delved into details unknown to me, expanded upon my existing knowledge, and even embarked on writing a self-help book. Beyond its role in calming anxiety, I found reading crucial in combatting anxiety through education.

How does education help with anxiety? For me, it's as undeniable as the fact that the earth is round: education is essential in battling anxiety. There's no way around it—only through. Terms like GAD, cognitive reframing, cognitive behavioral therapy (CBT), or dialectical behavior therapy (DBT) only came to my attention after my diagnosis and as I educated myself to alleviate my anxiety and manage my mental health. Education introduced me to healthy coping mechanisms and ideal role models for my mental health journey. It helped me understand the workings of my psyche, the influence of my life journey on my anxiety, and the significance of my emotions as indicators of deeper issues needing attention.

Reading connected me with others who shared my experiences, fostering empathy and leading me to communities with similar interests and hobbies. It made me a more engaging companion, positively affecting my social interactions and reducing my social anxiety. Education fueled my desire to help others, prompting me to start a psychology podcast. Sharing new learnings not only benefits me but also helps others understand topics like anxiety management techniques.

Education plays a crucial role in diminishing the stigma surrounding mental health. I emphasize that mental health should be treated with the same seriousness as physical health. Through education, we can dispel common misconceptions about mental health struggles, understanding that mental illness can affect anyone and should not be a source of judgment.

Educating oneself about symptoms and realizing that these experiences are either universal or unique to the individual can be incredibly empowering. My diagnosis of GAD, for instance, was a turning point, allowing me to research and understand my condition deeply. Knowing the range of treatment options—from medication and lifestyle changes to talk therapy—enables informed choices about managing anxiety. In my case, lifestyle adjustments proved most effective, differing from person to person in their impact.

Adopting a growth mindset is vital in motivating oneself to learn and believe in the possibility of healing through education and self-effort. This mindset is about embracing the potential for improvement and achieving goals (in this context, alleviating anxiety) through dedication and self-investment.

In this book, I aim to share everything I've learned about managing anxiety. This chapter will highlight selected resources that have been instrumental in my journey, detailing what has worked for me and what hasn't in the realm of education.

Books I Found Helpful:

- Retrain Your Brain: Cognitive Behavioral Therapy in 7 Weeks: A Workbook for Managing Depression and Anxiety
- Adult Children of Emotionally Immature Parents: How to Heal from Distant, Rejecting, or Self-Involved Parents
- Atomic Habits
- Be Calm: Proven Techniques to Stop Anxiety Now
- Declutter Your Mind: How to Stop Worrying, Relieve Anxiety, and Eliminate Negative Thinking
- Self-Love Workbook for Women: Release Self-Doubt, Build Self-Compassion, and Embrace Who You Are

Effective Therapy Treatments for Me:

- Talk therapy helped me intellectually understand my symptoms, with professionals guiding my education.
- CBT was transformative, altering my habits to foster a thriving life.

What Didn't Work for Me:

- Medications provided only temporary relief, leaving me feeling numb rather than rejuvenated.
- Group therapy, while supportive, sometimes overwhelmed me with others' emotional burdens.

Podcasts I Recommend:

- The Psychology of Your 20s
- Stanford Psychology Podcast
- Psychology Unplugged
- For those interested in exploring my podcast - Inquisitive Teaa Psychology is available on Spotify.

Scientific studies support the therapeutic effects of reading and education on mental health. For instance, a study in the Journal of Health Psychology has shown that engaging in reading can significantly reduce stress levels. Moreover, research underscores the importance of a growth mindset in overcoming challenges, as highlighted in Carol Dweck's work, suggesting that individuals who believe in their capacity to grow and learn are more likely to achieve success and overcome adversity, including anxiety (Dweck, 2006). This body of evidence reinforces the value of education and personal development in managing anxiety and enhancing overall well-being.

Chapter 10: The Power of Negativity

How can negativity be a force for good? Sounds paradoxical, right? But stick with me here. In the of chapters that precede this one, we have navigated the complex dance of radical acceptance, where we aim to embrace the hard truths about ourselves. These truths, often draped in shades of negativity, are not the enemies we often perceive them to be. I have come to see the so-called dark parts of myself not as pitfalls but as launchpads for growth; my personal shortcomings became the very steps I climbed to rise above my anxiety and enhance my emotional well-being.

The Art of Turning Influence into Inspiration

I am the kind of person who molds like clay in the hands of my environment; very easily influenced in other words. Surround me with naysayers, and I might start doubting the sun's warmth. But place me amidst mountain climbers, and before you know it, I'm reaching peaks both literal and metaphorical. It dawned on me that the power lay in my hands—to choose my influences wisely. This realization was my first victory in using negativity to my benefit. If being easily swayed was my Achilles' heel, I decided it would only sway me towards the light.

Screen Time: A Double-Edged Sword

Then there's the saga of screen time. In an era where screens are like extensions of our limbs, I found myself drowning in digital waves. But instead of letting this current pull me under, I turned the tide. I funneled my screen savvy into educational escapades—diving into online courses, devouring content that broadened my horizon, and embracing literature that taught me to dance in the rain of my anxiety.

From Physical Insecurities to Self-Empowerment

My journey with physical insecurities mirrors many. Yet, instead of wallowing in the quicksand of self-doubt, I chose action. Exercise and mindful eating became my rebellion against insecurity, transforming my reflection in the mirror into a source of pride, not pain.

Laziness: The Unlikely Muse

Ah, laziness—my familiar foe. It whispered sweet nothings of comfort and stagnation, luring me into a void of unachievement. But I saw through its guise. By embracing new hobbies and quenching my thirst for knowledge, I turned laziness on its head. Every new skill acquired, every page turned, became a testament to my victory over inertia.

People-Pleasing: A Double-Edged Gift

Let's talk about people-pleasing. Yes, it has led me down paths not my own, but it is also why I'm writing these words, why I started a podcast. I harnessed this trait, redirecting its energy towards endeavors that, while aiming to please, also fulfill a deeper purpose within me, and for others around me.

Embracing the Spectrum of Self

My motto? "Make friends with your enemies." This philosophy transformed my inner turmoil into a wellspring of peace. Each trait, each perceived flaw, became a tool in my fight against anxiety, propelling me towards a version of myself unburdened by the weight of negativity.

Research supports the notion that acknowledging and working with our negative traits can foster personal growth. Studies in the field of psychology, such as those published in the Journal of Personality and Social Psychology, suggest that self-acceptance and understanding one's weaknesses are crucial for psychological well-being. Additionally, cognitive-behavioral therapy (CBT) principles, which involve recognizing and changing negative thought patterns, have been shown to effectively reduce anxiety and improve mental health outcomes, as documented in research within the American Journal of Psychiatry.

Negativity, when acknowledged and harnessed correctly, can indeed be a powerful force for personal development, emotional resilience, and anxiety reduction, as exemplified by my personal anecdotes.

Chapter 11: Power of No Power

Embracing Vulnerability Amid Mental Health Struggles

Often, while grappling with anxiety or other mental health challenges, we might project a facade of wellness, convincing ourselves that we need to simply "toughen up" and push through. This approach, however, is flawed. While pretending to be fine might offer temporary relief, failing to acknowledge and be true to our feelings traps us in a state of denial, delaying our progress toward a healthier mental state.

The Essence of Vulnerability

I've come to understand what I call "the power of having no power" as the strength found in vulnerability. The stigma surrounding mental health issues is so pervasive that many of us end up stigmatizing ourselves. Thoughts like "Why am I depressed when everything in my life is good?" signify a denial and lack of vulnerability deeply rooted in self-stigma. This issue is compounded in cultures where mental health stigma is rampant, amplifying self-stigma and exacerbating anxiety and mental health woes.

My own journey was marked by secrecy and shame. Diagnosed and prescribed medication, I hid my treatment from family and friends, struggling to accept that I needed help. This resistance stemmed from a deep-seated self-stigma, a reluctance to be perceived as weak for battling mental health issues.

The Stigma of Seeking Help

In my homeland, Myanmar, the search for therapy is often mocked, and mental health care is stigmatized, casting those who seek help as societal outliers. This public stigma leads many to internalize societal views, making it difficult to exercise free will in seeking help or expressing struggles, reinforcing the feeling of isolation.

Vulnerability as Liberation

True freedom comes when we lower our defenses, allowing ourselves to be seen in our authentic struggles. Advocating for mental health, I emphasize that it's not a sign of weakness but a human condition that merits the same attention and care as physical health. By openly discussing my diagnosis and affirming that it's okay not to be okay, I've paved the way for others to feel understood and less alone.

Challenging Gendered Stigma

The stigma is particularly tenacious for men, who are often encouraged to "man up." Recognizing and accepting emotional struggles as a normal aspect of human experience can dismantle this harmful narrative. Life, with its myriad challenges, rarely allows us to maintain constant emotional stability. Acknowledging vulnerability not only fosters self-acceptance but also advocates for broader societal understanding.

Vulnerability and Connection

My vulnerability has placed me in a win-win situation. Negative reactions prompt me to educate or establish boundaries, while positive ones lead to shared experiences and stronger connections.

This openness has guided me toward effective therapy, supportive communities, and creative outlets like writing and podcasting.

Research supports the benefits of vulnerability. Studies, such as those in the Journal of Clinical Psychology, suggest that embracing vulnerability can significantly improve mental health outcomes. Vulnerability allows for genuine self-expression, fostering environments where support and understanding can thrive, thereby reducing the felt stigma and promoting healing.

In essence, the power of having no power — embracing vulnerability — is a profound tool for mental health advocacy and personal growth. It transforms our struggles into opportunities for connection, understanding, and healing, illustrating that vulnerability is not a weakness but a courageous step toward authenticity and wellness.

Afterword

Having journeyed through my own experiences with Generalized Anxiety Disorder (GAD) as detailed in this book, I've distilled my learnings and coping mechanisms into eleven chapters, each a step towards managing and understanding GAD better. This epilogue, therefore, is not just a summary but a reflection from a deeply personal standpoint, acknowledging the struggles, the strategies to overcome them, and the continuous path to recovery and empowerment. It encapsulates the essence of each chapter, highlighting the key takeaways and how they've shaped my understanding and management of anxiety. Through this journey, I've learned the importance of self-awareness, acceptance, and the use of practical tools to power through GAD, aiming to share these insights to help others navigate their own paths with greater ease and confidence.

References

Benet-Martínez, V., Leu, J., Lee, F., & Morris, M.W. (2002). Negotiating biculturalism: Cultural frame switching in biculturals with oppositional versus compatible cultural identities. Journal of Cross-Cultural Psychology, 33(5), 492-516. DOI: 10.1177/0022022102033005005

Crocker, J., & Park, L.E. (2004). The costly pursuit of self-esteem. Psychological Bulletin, 130(3), 392-414. DOI: 10.1037/0033-2909.130.3.392

Dweck, C.S. (2006). Mindset: The new psychology of success. Random House.

Kashdan, T.B., & Rottenberg, J. (2010). Psychological flexibility as a fundamental aspect of health. Clinical Psychology Review, 30(7), 865-878. DOI: 10.1016/j.cpr.2010.03.001

Masten, A.S. (2001). Ordinary magic: Resilience processes in development. American Psychologist, 56(3), 227-238. DOI: 10.1037//0003-066X.56.3.227

Neff, K.D. (2003). The development and validation of a scale to measure self-compassion. Self and Identity, 2(3), 223-250. DOI: 10.1080/15298860309027

Neff, K.D., & Vonk, R. (2009). Self-compassion versus global self-esteem: Two different ways of relating to oneself. Journal of Personality, 77(1), 23-50. DOI: 10.1111/j.1467-6494.2008.00537.x

Ryan, R.M., & Deci, E.L. (2000). Self-determination theory and the facilitation of intrinsic motivation, social development, and well-being. American Psychologist, 55(1), 68-78. DOI: 10.1037//0003-066X.55.1.68

Seligman, M.E.P., Steen, T.A., Park, N., & Peterson, C. (2005). Positive psychology progress: Empirical validation of interventions. American Psychologist, 60(5), 410-421. DOI: 10.1037/0003-066X.60.5.410

Wood, A.M., Froh, J.J., & Geraghty, A.W.A. (2010). Gratitude and well-being: A review and theoretical integration. Clinical Psychology Review, 30(7), 890-905. DOI: 10.1016/j.cpr.2010.03.005

Brown, Brené. Daring Greatly: How the Courage to Be Vulnerable Transforms the Way We Live, Love, Parent, and Lead. Gotham Books, 2012.

Gilbert, Paul. The Compassionate Mind: A New Approach to Life's Challenges. New Harbinger Publications, 2009.

Neff, Kristin D. Self-Compassion: The Proven Power of Being Kind to Yourself. William Morrow, 2011.

Corrigan, Patrick W., and Amy C. Watson. "Understanding the Impact of Stigma on People with Mental Illness." World Psychiatry, vol. 1, no. 1, 2002, pp. 16–20.

American Psychological Association. The Road to Resilience. American Psychological Association, 2014, http://www.apa.org/helpcenter/road-resilience.aspx.

Hedeker, Donald, and Robert D. Gibbons. "A Random-Effects Ordinal Regression Model for Multilevel Analysis." Biometrics, vol. 50, no. 4, 1994, pp. 933–944.

Printed in Great Britain
by Amazon